HOW TO BECOME
AN ENTREPRENEUR

EDUARD BOECKMANN

Disclaimer: By accepting, borrowing, buying, or reading this book you agree that you are fully and solely responsible for any actions you take as a result of reading any information contained in this book.

Professional Advice and Publisher's Responsibilities

This document is written to provide exact and reliable information for educational purposes in regard to the subject and the issues covered herein. The publication is sold with the understanding that the publisher is not required to render any accounting, officially permitted, or otherwise qualified services.

If advice is necessary, legal or professional, a practiced individual in the profession should be consulted.

From a Declaration of Principles which was accepted and

approved equally by a Committee of the American Bar Association and a Committee of Publishers and Associations, the following has been declared:

This book is dedicated to my family and friends.

TABLE OF CONTENTS

NOTHING WORTHWHILE IS EASILY ACHIEVED!

1. Define what becoming an entrepreneur is

Becoming an entrepreneur requires skills such as creativity, innovation, strategic thinking, risk-taking, and leadership.

Successful entrepreneurs are able to navigate through challenges and uncertainties, and adapt to changes in the market, while staying true to their vision and goals.

Entrepreneurship is often associated with small businesses and startups, but it can also occur within larger organizations, where employees are encouraged to think creatively and take on new projects.

The benefits of entrepreneurship include the potential for financial success, job creation, and the ability to make a positive impact on society through innovation and problem-solving.

2. Describe what a possible starting point would be for a person wanting to be an entrepreneur.

If you're interested in becoming an entrepreneur, here are a few possible starting points you might consider:

Identify a problem or need: One way to start a business is to identify a problem or need in the market and create a product or service that solves that problem or fills that need.

3. What kinds of new products or services are in most need today to supply or create for an entrepreneur?

There are several new products or services that are in high demand today and could potentially be lucrative for entrepreneurs.

Here are a few examples: E-commerce platforms: With the

rise of online shopping and the COVID-19 pandemic forcing many businesses to shift their focus to online sales, there is a high demand for e-commerce platforms that are easy to use, customizable, and affordable.

Remote work tools: As more and more people work from home or remotely, there is a growing need for tools and services that enable remote collaboration, communication, and project management.

Health and wellness products/services: With an increasing focus on health and wellness, there is a high demand for products and services that help people maintain a healthy lifestyle.

This includes everything from fitness apps to healthy meal delivery services.

Sustainability-focused products/services: With growing concern for the environment, there is a demand for products and services that help people live a more sustainable lifestyle, such as eco-friendly cleaning products, electric cars, and sustainable fashion brands.

Personalized experiences: There is a trend towards personalization in many industries, including retail, travel, and entertainment. Entrepreneurs who can provide personalized experiences, such as customized clothing or personalized travel itineraries, may find success in this space.

Entrepreneurs should research their target market and stay up-to-date with trends to identify new opportunities.

Note that consumer locations and culture can affect their needs and choices when purchasing goods or services.

4. What are skills that an entrepreneur should have for success?

Here are some important skills that an entrepreneur should have:

Creativity and Innovation: Entrepreneurs should be able to

think outside the box, come up with new ideas, and innovate.

Be able to do research and identify good opportunities, market needs.

Risk-taking: Be willing to take reasonable calculated risks.

Resilient: Be able to handle stress. Recover quickly from failures and setbacks, pivoting if necessary to go around some problems.

Adaptable: Be able to handle changes, overcome obstacles, and be willing to take care of a lot of details every day.

Finances: Be able to handle finances, planning and budgeting, accounting, record keeping.

Have strong interpersonal skills. Make friends and keep them available to you. It is amazing how much other people with insight can help you with suggestions and ideas!

Leadership: Be able to lead and motivate people. This is perhaps the most important thing to build a successful business. Work on this with your people every day!

Network: Be able to build strong relationship with the movers and shakers in their field, and anyone who is important to know for help and ideas.

Be able to communicate effectively: This includes being able to articulate their vision and ideas clearly, actively listening, and responding appropriately.

The above are the usual basic requirements to be a successful entrepreneur, but there also be other skill needs that are required to be able to start a business in a particular field. For example, if you are starting a software business, you should at least know some basic computing coding, partner with someone who is capable in software development.

5. What are the first steps a new entrepreneur should take to get started with his business?

Identify a business idea. This is the crucial step to find something that you can do with your business and be successful!

Do market research. If you cannot do the research yourself, find a service that can do it for you. You may need to do this if the research requires a review of "big data" pools, that requires some heavy- duty computer work.

Assess the viability of your business: This could involve researching the competition, determining the target market, and evaluating potential demand.

Develop a business plan: A well-written business plan is essential for securing funding and guiding the direction of the business. It should contain the following elements:

Description of the business, what, where, when, and how, real estate and buildings required, space required, equipment required. Date of start-up. Cash required to start.

Marketing strategies, what market, what product or service, how to penetrate the market, pricing.

Financial projections, investment, revenue, profit margin, cash required.

An operations plan, what happens, who does each task, what is the sequence of actions, who supervises, milestones, dates, include flow charts.

Secure funding (e.g., personal funds, loans, grants, letters of credit, etc.)

Register the business in your location, state, city, county as applicable: Get licenses, permits, and register your company for taxes with your state and Federal government.

Some states have various requirements, so you should find out what our state's rules are for business formation, reports, and taxation requirements.

Set up the business infrastructure: This may involve setting up a physical location, establishing a website, creating a social media presence, and hiring employees if necessary.

Launch the business: Finally, it is time to launch the business and start selling products or services to customers. It is important to continue to monitor the business and make adjustments as necessary to ensure long-term success.

6. If a person decides to become an entrepreneur, how should he be mentally prepared to be successful?

Becoming an entrepreneur requires a significant mental and emotional investment. Here are some ways to mentally prepare for success as an entrepreneur:

Be ready to deal the unknown. There are always things that can and will happen when a person is starting a business, and even when it appears to be running smoothly without a problem.

Be ready for unexpected challenges. Have the attitude that you will overcome anything that might happen to discourage you, or seem to stop you. You need to decide that you will be successful no matter what happens!

Develop a growth mindset. Almost all businesses start small. In order to really be successful your business needs to steadily grow until your business is profitable and provides a good income for you and your stockholders or members of your company.

Be able to do hard work. Rewards from doing business will not just fall into your account. Any real successful business will take many hours of hard work. There is no free lunch in business!

Have perseverance. Don't get easily discouraged and quit. Yes, there will be failures causing you to step back and make corrections. But remember your business will only fail if you quit! If you lose your market due to changes outside of your control, find a new market for another product or service and keep going!

Stay focused on your goals. Don't get distracted by some "pie in the sky" scheme or proposal, stay with your business and keep working at it.

Keep in mind what you want to achieve, and take steps every day to move closer to your objectives. Be resilient: Entrepreneurship can be a rollercoaster ride of highs and lows.

Understand the potential risks of your business before you start it. Also know what your rewards will be when it is operating. What is your profit margin? Are you able to make a satisfactory income for your work building and operating the business?

Stay motivated: You will need to stay motivated and passionate about your work to overcome the challenges you will face. Find ways to stay inspired and maintain your enthusiasm for your business.

Build a strong support system. This could be partners or people who you know can do the work and be an asset to your company.

Consult with people who are knowledgeable in your field of work. Keep an open mind to the views of people in your circle of contacts and the people you are working with.

Find experts who have the knowledge you need and can give you good advice about what to do when!

In the following sections we will discuss some things that are recommended to do once your business is formed and operating.

7. Periodic self-evaluations

There are several ways an entrepreneur can evaluate themselves and their business:

Reviewing financial performance: One of the most important ways to evaluate your business is to assess its financial performance. You can track revenue, expenses, profit margins, and other key financial metrics to determine how well your business is doing.

Assessing customer satisfaction: Customer satisfaction is crucial for any business. Measure customer satisfaction by gathering feedback through surveys, customer ratings, and social media. If your customers are happy, that is a good sign.

Evaluating market share: Another way to evaluate your business is to analyze your market share. You can look at your market share relative to your competitors to determine how well you are doing in your industry.

Are you keeping your employees? If not try to find out why. Are you making progress against your goals? Are you achieving your goals, or are you off track?

By doing the above things you should know where you need to make correction or changes.

Overall, it's important for entrepreneurs to regularly evaluate their business using a combination of financial, customer, and employee metrics, as well as by setting goals and tracking progress.

8. Review employee performance

Evaluating employees is an important task for any entrepreneur, as it helps to ensure that their team is performing at a high level and contributing to the success of the business.

Here are some steps an entrepreneur can take to evaluate their employees effectively:

Set clear expectations: Before evaluating an employee's performance, it's important to establish clear expectations about what their role entails and what they are expected to achieve. Create a job description that specifies the job duties and allows you to evaluate the employee's performance.

Use objective criteria: When evaluating an employee, it's important to use objective criteria that are based on measurable outcomes, rather than subjective opinions or impressions. It could be things like sales numbers, projects completed on time, etc.

Recognize and reward good performance: When an employee performs well, it's important to recognize their achievements and reward them appropriately. Rewards could be salary increases, stock options, paid holidays, etc.

Be sure to address any performance issues accurately so the employee understands exactly where he or she needs to improve. Provide any help that you can.

By following these steps, an entrepreneur can evaluate their employees in a fair and effective manner, which can help to build a strong and productive team that contributes to the success of the business.

9. How should an entrepreneur evaluate his business periodically?

Here are some steps you can take to review your business periodically.

Set specific goals and objectives: Before you begin the review process, set clear goals and objectives that you want to achieve.

Gather relevant data: Collect all the necessary data that will help you evaluate your business performance. This may include financial statements, sales reports, customer feedback, employee performance metrics, and other relevant information.

Analyze the data: Once you have gathered the data, analyze it to identify any trends, patterns, or areas of concern. Look for areas where you may be falling short of your goals, as well as areas where you are doing well.

Make adjustments: Based on the insights you have gained from the review process, make adjustments to your business strategy, operations, or marketing efforts as needed. Implement any changes that will help you achieve your goals more effectively.

Monitor the results and get feedback from customers and employees.

By following these steps, you can conduct a thorough review of your business periodically and make informed decisions that will help you achieve your goals and grow your business over time.

10. How to award employees for good performance.

Entrepreneurs can reward their employees in various ways for jobs well done.

Here are some ideas:

Monetary Rewards: This can include bonuses, raises, profit-sharing, or stock options.

Non-Monetary Rewards: These can include flexible work schedules, additional vacation days, or work from home options.

Professional Development Opportunities: Providing employees with opportunities for training, attending conferences, or continuing education courses can show that you value their growth and development.

Employee Perks: Offering discounts on products or services, gym memberships, gift cards, special reward plaques, framed certificates of achievement, or other benefits can be a great way to reward employees.

Personalized Rewards: Tailoring rewards to an employee's individual interests or preferences can show that you care about them on a personal level.

Public recognition: A company announcement, compliments in a meeting, public posters. A meeting set up with the boss when an award plaque or certificate may be presented.

Team Outings: Organizing a fun outing or event for the team can be a great way to build morale and reward employees for their hard work.

It's important to remember that what works as a reward for one employee may not be effective for another. Therefore, it's essential to get to know your employees and what motivates them so you can tailor rewards accordingly.

10 RULES FOR WORKPLACE SAFETY

1. You are responsible for your own safety and for the safety of others.
2. All accidents are preventable.
3. Do not take short cuts. Always follow the rules.
4. If you are not trained, don't do it.
5. Use the right tools & equipment and use them in the right way
6. Assess the risks before you approach your work.
7. Never wear loose clothes or slippery footwear.
8. Do not indulge in horseplay while at work.
9. Practice good housekeeping.
10. Always wear PPEs.

11.   What general safety rules, practices, and

equipment should be incorporated in the business?

Incorporating safety rules, practices, and equipment is essential to ensure the safety and well-being of employees, customers, and visitors in a business setting.

Here are some general guidelines to follow:

Conduct a risk assessment: Identify potential hazards in the workplace and assess the risk associated with them. Develop safety policies and procedures: Develop clear and concise safety policies and procedures that employees can follow.

Regularly review and update training programs to reflect changes in equipment, technology, and processes.

Use personal protective equipment (PPE): Provide and require the use of PPE, such as helmets, safety glasses, gloves, and respirators, as appropriate to the work being performed.

Establish emergency procedures: Develop and implement emergency procedures for evacuations, fire, first aid, and other potential emergencies.

Promote good housekeeping: Maintain a clean, organized, and clutter-free workplace to reduce the risk of slips, trips, and falls.

Encourage open communication: Encourage employees to report safety concerns and hazards, and establish a process for addressing these concerns promptly.

Set up procedures to eliminate risks by proper operating procedures and practices.

Clearly communicate safety policies to employees.

Do periodic safety training for all employees.

Establish periodic maintenance schedules for equipment.

Do a periodic "walk though" inspection of all areas to verify safety practices are followed.

Make sure all buildings where employees work or where hazardous materials are stored are equipped with safety devices such as fire detector alarms, sprinklers, and any other safety devices that might be needed depending on the type of product, service, or building code requirements.

KNOW THE ENVIRONMENTAL LAWS AND TESTING.

12. Environmental compliance

To ensure compliance with environmental regulations, a company should take the following steps:

Research the applicable regulations: Companies should determine which environmental regulations apply to their industry and operations. This research can be conducted by reviewing government websites, consulting with regulatory agencies, and seeking legal counsel.

Develop a compliance plan: Once a company understands which regulations apply to their operations, they should develop a compliance plan to meet those requirements.

Train employees: Employees who work in areas that are affected by environmental regulations should receive training on the company's compliance plan and procedures.

Monitor compliance: The company should regularly monitor its operations to ensure that it is complying with all relevant regulations. This can include testing for pollutants, reviewing data logs, and inspecting equipment to ensure that it is functioning properly.

Maintain records: The company should keep detailed records of its compliance activities, including monitoring results, permits, and other documentation.

Seek professional help: Companies can also seek the assistance of environmental consultants or legal counsel who specialize in environmental regulations to ensure compliance. These professionals can provide guidance on the specific requirements and help the company develop a compliance plan that meets all regulatory requirements.

13.   Check and improve working conditions

First review what the working conditions are for each job. Ask the employee if there is anything about their job that gives them trouble, wastes time, that they think is wrong, or that they do not like.

Study how the conditions for that job can be improved and then implement changes and re-check the conditions for the job.

Improving working conditions can involve a variety of strategies depending on the specific context and industry. However, here are some general tips:

Provide a safe and healthy working environment: This includes ensuring proper ventilation, adequate lighting, ergonomic furniture, and regular cleaning and maintenance of the workspace.

Encourage work-life balance: This includes offering flexible schedules, remote work options, and opportunities for employees to take breaks or recharge during the workday.

Provide opportunities for professional growth: This includes offering training and development programs, mentorship, and opportunities for advancement within the company.

Address any specific concerns or issues that employees may have: This can involve conducting regular surveys to gather feedback, addressing any grievances in a timely and respectful manner, and ensuring that employees feel heard and valued.

Make sure that the pay and benefits are fair and competitive for each job relative to your industry. Basic benefits are health insurance, paid time off, and retirement plans.

Make employees feel valued and respected.

Allow employees freedom to directly communicate with management at all times for any complaints or comments and keep employees up-to-date with important developments that might affect them, to foster an open atmosphere for employees.

Emphasize teamwork wherever possible to give employees a sense of support and provide employee counseling and problem support to eliminate any feeling that they are alone with no support. Provide each employee with a mentor or a support person who is available to help them when needed.

By implementing these strategies, employers can help to create a positive and productive work environment that benefits both the employees and the company as a whole.

Type of Account	Debit	Credit
Asset A/C	Increase	Decrease
Liability A/C	Decrease	Increase
Capital A/C	Decrease	Increase
Revenue A/C	Decrease	Increase
Expenses A/C	Increase	Decrease
Drawings A/C	Increase	Decrease

14. What kind of an accounting system should be used?

The type of accounting system that a company should use depends on various factors, including the nature of the business, the size of the company, and its specific needs and goals.

In general, both a company that provides a physical product and a company that provides only a service will need to use some form of accounting system to manage their finances effectively and comply with relevant laws and regulations.

For a company that provides a physical product, a comprehensive inventory management system is crucial to keep track of the stock levels, reorder points, and costs of goods sold.

An accounting system that integrates with the inventory management system can help ensure accurate and timely financial statements and facilitate effective decision-making.

On the other hand, a company that provides only a service may not require an inventory management system, but it will need to track its service revenue, expenses, and profitability.

In this case, a standard accounting system with modules for tracking expenses, invoicing, and accounts receivable and payable may be sufficient.

In both cases, the accounting system should be able to generate financial statements and reports that provide valuable insights into the company's financial health and performance. It's important to choose an accounting system that fits the company's needs and is scalable as the business grows and evolves.

When filing taxes, you will need to complete Schedule C on your tax return. So, you should remember that requirement when setting up your accounting system. Schedule C requires certain data that your accounting system will need to provide.

TO GROW, BRANCH OUT!

15. Expand the business

Expanding a business through branching out with new products and services can be a great way for an entrepreneur to grow their business.

Here are some steps to consider:

Research: Start by researching the market and identifying opportunities for new products or services that complement your existing offerings or fill a gap in the market.

Evaluate: Consider the resources needed to develop and launch the new product or service, such as time, money, and staff.

Evaluate the potential return on investment and determine whether it is a viable option for your business.

Develop a plan: Create a detailed plan that outlines the steps needed to bring the new product or service to market, including production, marketing, and sales.

Test: Before launching the new product or service, test it with a small group of customers or in a limited market to gauge its viability and gather feedback.

Launch: Once you have refined the product or service and are confident in its potential success, launch it to a wider audience using targeted marketing strategies.

Monitor and adjust: Monitor the performance of the new product or service and make adjustments as needed to ensure its ongoing success.

This may include adjusting pricing, marketing strategies, or even the product itself based on customer feedback.

By following these steps, an entrepreneur can successfully branch out with new products and services and expand their business.

16.   Risk analysis

Risk analysis is an important process for any entrepreneur looking to start or grow a business.

It involves identifying potential risks and uncertainties that could impact the success of the business, and developing strategies to mitigate those risks.

Here are some steps an entrepreneur can take to perform risk analysis and prepare for eventualities:

Identify potential risks: The first step in risk analysis is to identify potential risks that could impact the business.

These could include financial risks, such as changes in the economy or unexpected expenses, legal risks, such as lawsuits or regulatory changes, operational risks, such as equipment failure.

Also, there could be supply chain disruptions, and reputational risks, such as negative press or customer complaints.

Evaluate the likelihood and impact of each risk: Once potential risks have been identified, the entrepreneur should evaluate the likelihood and potential impact of each risk.

This can be done by considering factors such as the probability of the risk occurring, the potential financial or operational impact, and the time it would take to recover from the risk.

Develop risk mitigation strategies:

Based on the evaluation of each risk, the entrepreneur should develop risk mitigation strategies.

These could include implementing financial safeguards, such as building a cash reserve or securing additional financing, creating contingency plans for unexpected events, such as having backup suppliers or alternative revenue streams.

Develop crisis communication plans to address reputational risks.

Monitor and update risk analysis:

Risk analysis is an ongoing process, and the entrepreneur should monitor and update their risk analysis regularly to ensure that their business remains prepared for eventualities.

This could involve reviewing financial statements and industry trends, staying up-to-date on regulatory changes, and evaluating the effectiveness of risk mitigation strategies.

Overall, risk analysis is a critical process for entrepreneurs to help them identify and prepare for potential risks to their business.

By evaluating potential risks, developing mitigation strategies, and monitoring their business regularly, entrepreneurs can better position themselves to succeed and overcome any challenges that may arise.

17.   What are the advantages of a Limited Liability Corporation (LLC)?

Setting up a Limited Liability Company (LLC) can offer several advantages to business owners.

Here are some of the key benefits:

Limited personal liability: One of the primary advantages of an

LLC is that it limits the personal liability of the owners.

In other words, if the LLC incurs debts or legal issues, the personal assets of the owners (such as their homes or personal savings) are generally protected.

This protection is not absolute, but it can be a significant advantage over sole proprietorships or partnerships, where the owners have unlimited personal liability.

Flexibility in taxation: LLCs offer flexibility in how they are taxed. By default, an LLC is taxed as a pass-through entity, meaning that the profits and losses are reported on the individual tax returns of the owners.

However, an LLC can also choose to be taxed as a corporation, which may be more advantageous depending on the specific circumstances of the business.

Simplified management structure: LLCs are relatively easy to set up and manage compared to other business structures, such as corporations.

They have fewer formal requirements and do not require a board of directors or annual shareholder meetings.

This simplicity can save time and money for the owners.

Increased credibility: Setting up an LLC can increase the credibility of a business, particularly if it is a new or small business.

Customers, vendors, and potential partners may view an LLC as a more professional and trustworthy entity than a sole proprietorship or partnership.

Ownership flexibility: LLCs offer flexibility in ownership, allowing for multiple owners (known as "members") with different ownership percentages.

This can be particularly advantageous for businesses with multiple partners or investors.

Overall, setting up an LLC can provide several benefits for business owners, including limited personal liability, tax flexibility, simplified management structure, increased credibility, and ownership flexibility.

However, it's important to consult with a legal and financial professional to determine if an LLC is the right structure for your specific business needs.

18.   Transfer of ownership

There are several ways an entrepreneur can transfer ownership of their company to someone else in the event of their retirement or death.

Here are a few common methods: Sale to a third party: The entrepreneur can sell their company to a third party, such as a competitor, a private equity firm, or another entrepreneur.

The sale can be structured as an outright purchase or a sale of shares in the company.

Transfer of ownership to family members. This can be done through gifting or selling shares of the company to the family members.

Transfer to employees: Employee Stock Ownership Plan (ESOP). An ESOP is a retirement plan that invests primarily in the employer's stock, giving employees an ownership stake in the company.

Succession planning: The entrepreneur can develop a succession plan, which outlines how the company will be transferred to a new owner.

This plan can include identifying and training a successor, determining a timeline for the transfer of ownership, and outlining the financial terms of the transfer.

It's important for entrepreneurs to work with a team of professionals, including lawyers, accountants, and financial advisors, to ensure that the ownership transfer is done correctly and legally.

They should also communicate their wishes to their family members, employees, and other stakeholders, to ensure a smooth transition of ownership in the event of retirement or death.

19.   A general list of actions to complete

Here is a general list of actions that an entrepreneur should perform to form a business:

Identify the business idea: The first step is to identify a viable business idea that solves a problem or meets a need in the market.

Research the market .

Create a business plan.

Choose a business structure.

Register the business.

Secure funding.

Set up a business bank account.

Develop a branding strategy.

Create a brand name, logo, and marketing strategy to promote the business.

Hire employees or contractors: If necessary, hire employees or contractors to help run the business.

Set up accounting and record-keeping systems: Establish a system for accounting and record-keeping to ensure the financial health of the business.

Launch the business: Once all the necessary steps have been completed, launch the business and start serving customers.

Consult with legal and financial professionals if needed.

20. Ten rules for success

1. Set clear goals: Know exactly what you want to achieve and create a plan to get there.
2. Take action: Success requires taking consistent, focused action towards your goals.
3. Stay motivated: Keep yourself inspired and focused on your goals, even when things get tough.
4. Learn from failure: Mistakes and setbacks are inevitable, but they provide valuable opportunities for learning and growth.
5. Develop good habits.
6. Be persistent.
7. Learn and improve.

8. Keep good friends with positive influences.
9. Manage your time.
10.   Be adaptable.

21.   Change your mindset.

How can a person change their mindset to be a successful entrepreneur?

Changing one's mindset to become a successful entrepreneur requires a combination of self-reflection, learning, and adopting certain attitudes and behaviors. Here are some key steps you can take:

Embrace a Growth Mindset: A growth mindset is the belief that skills and abilities can be developed through dedication and hard work.

Understand that entrepreneurship is a learning process, and setbacks and failures are opportunities for growth and improvement.

Develop Self-Awareness: Gain a deep understanding of your strengths, weaknesses, passions, and values. Identify the areas where you excel and the areas that need improvement.

Self-awareness will help you make better decisions and leverage your strengths effectively.

Set Clear Goals: Define your long-term vision and set specific, measurable, attainable, relevant, and time-bound intelligent goals. Break them down into smaller milestones, allowing you to track your progress and maintain motivation.

Adopt a Positive Attitude: Cultivate a positive mindset by focusing on solutions rather than problems.

See challenges as opportunities and setbacks as learning experiences. Surround yourself with positive and supportive people who believe in your vision.

Take Calculated Risks: Entrepreneurship involves taking risks, but it's important to take calculated and informed risks. Evaluate the potential rewards and potential consequences before making decisions.

Develop a tolerance for uncertainty and learn to manage and mitigate risks effectively.

Continuously Learn: Invest in your education and personal development.

Read books, attend seminars, join entrepreneurship networks, and learn from successful entrepreneurs.

Stay updated on industry trends and emerging technologies to adapt and innovate.

Build Resilience: Entrepreneurship can be demanding and challenging.

Develop resilience by maintaining a positive mindset, practicing self-care, and seeking support when needed. Learn from failures, adapt quickly, and persevere in the face of obstacles.

Network and Collaborate: Build a strong network of like-minded individuals, mentors, and experts.

Attend industry events, join entrepreneurial communities, and seek opportunities to collaborate.

Surround yourself with people who can offer guidance, support, and valuable connections.

Take Action and Iterate: Avoid analysis paralysis and take action.

Start with a minimum viable product (MVP) or prototype and gather feedback from your target audience. Iterate and refine your product or service based on the feedback received, allowing you to adapt to market needs.

Stay Flexible and Open-Minded: Be willing to pivot and adapt your business strategy based on feedback, market conditions, and emerging opportunities.

Stay open-minded, embrace change, and continuously seek innovative solutions.

Remember, changing your mindset takes time and effort.

It's a continuous journey of self-improvement and growth.

Stay committed, persevere through challenges, and remain focused on your long-term goals.

Some related books

HARNESS THE POWER OF THE SUBCONSCIOUS: YOU

by Eduard Boeckmann | Apr 22, 2023

Kindle

$0⁰⁰ kindleunlimited

Included with your Kindle Unlimited membership Learn More

Available instantly

Read for Free

Or $2.99 to buy

Paperback

$7⁷⁵

✓prime

FREE delivery **Tue, May 16**

YOU CAN BE SUCCESSFUL IN BUSINESS!

HOW TO SET UP AND OPERATE YOUR BUSINESS

EDUARD BOECKMANN

You can be Successful in Business: How to set up

by EDUARD BOECKMANN | Apr 17, 2023

★★★★★ ~ 1

Kindle

$0⁰⁰ kindleunlimited

Included with your Kindle Unlimited membership Learn More

Available instantly

Read for Free

Or $2.99 to buy

Paperback

$5⁷⁵

✓prime

FREE delivery **Mon, May 15**

CHANGE YOUR MINDSET FOR SUCCESS!

by Eduard Boeckmann | May 4, 2023

Kindle

$0⁰⁰ kindleunlimited

Included with your Kindle Unlimited
membership Learn More

Available instantly

Read for Free

Or $2.99 to buy

Paperback

$7⁹⁵

✓prime
FREE delivery **Tue, May 16**